A Blueprint For a Highly Successful Life

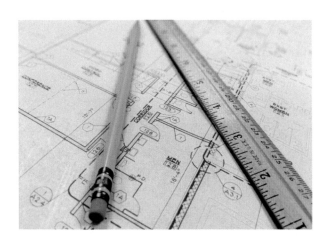

A Survival Guide For the Aftermath Of the COVID-19 Pandemic

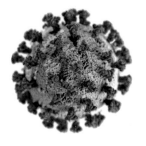

Dr. Tom McCawley

Published by Bristlecone Publishing, Lakewood, Colorado

Printed in the United States of America.

ISBN: 978-0-9855111-6-6

Required Disclaimer

This publication is designed to provide accurate and authoritative information regarding the subject matter covered. It is sold with the understanding that the author and the publisher are not engaged in rendering medical, psychological, legal, accounting, or other professional services. If legal advice or other expert assistance is required, the services of a competent professional person should be sought.

50% of the profit from this book will be donated to enhancing dental education and reducing its cost.

If you have comments or questions,
you may contact Dr. McCawley at
tom@mcawley.com.

This Book is Dedicated to
The Ones I Love
As a Legacy of Joy and Hope

My wife, Brenda, an incredible supporter and inspiration

My four sons, Tom, Paul, Dan and Mark

My brother Dan, his wife Carol, and their family

My two daughters-in-law, Sigrid and Suzanne

My seven grandchildren,
Sam, Patrick, Evelyn, Kincaid, Max, Zac, and Maddy

My team members in my practice-
"The Dream Team," my second family

And finally, this book is dedicated to
all those who have struggled with life
during the COVID-19 crisis,
and other crises — which is all of us!

Acknowledgements

Wind on My Back!

Wow! I could write a book about my gratitude to all those who have been wind on my back.

The place to start is with my wife Brenda. Your spouse can be either wind on your back, or a pit bull on your leg. My wife has been a hurricane on my back.

My four boys, Tom, Paul, Dan, and Mark, have also inspired me by giving my life purpose, and by becoming such wonderful human beings, despite my many *mess*takes* as a parent.

****mess*takes—mistakes, not learned from
and repeated, create life's messes.**

Maybe Webster's will add this new word to their next edition?

My mom, Delta, taught me to learn from others' *mess*takes, and my dad, Byron, taught me what *mess*takes to avoid. I will share my parents' wisdom and Solomon's Proverbs frequently in the text. This proverb certainly applies to me:

"Listen, my child, to what your father teaches you.
Don't neglect your mother's teachings.
What you learn from them will crown you with grace
and clothe you with honor."
Proverbs 1:8, 9

My editor and friends, Ann Nye West, and her husband, Jim, were extremely helpful in making my ideas more readable and organized.

Table of Contents

What Others Say About Why You Should Read This Book

"Don't praise yourself; let others do it!"
Proverbs 27:2

"Dr. Tom McCawley has penned a true guide for the times. This quick, but powerful read gives practical and easy-to-implement advice for today's uncertain times. For all of us who are trying to navigate a truly unprecedented chapter in our lives, this is an absolute gem that should be kept in your back pocket and read multiple times."

Corey Perlman
Digital Marketing Speaker & Consultant
Atlanta, Georgia

"Over almost 20 years of advising families, I came to believe that a person's true character is ultimately revealed in the quality of their decision-making. Not all of us get it right the first time, but steady progress in our ability to choose between competing alternatives is essential to a life of significance and purpose. It's been my privilege, over the years, to observe Tom and Brenda McCawley's demonstrated ability to make difficult choices that result in enduring benefits to their family, their co-workers, their patients, and their profession. I can readily attest that the principles Tom offers have been tested through their ongoing application in his own life. Dr. McCawley's book represents a distilling of years of personal and professional experience into a gift of immeasurable value to those with ears to hear."

Robert E. Baker
Senior Financial Advisor
Ronald Blue & Co.
Orlando, Florida

"Tom McCawley looks like Clark Kent, but when he grabs a microphone or a pen, he turns into Superman! He brings a unique combination of both being very practical and truly inspirational. I highly recommend his book to all who want more rewarding and fulfilled lives."

Michael A. Chizner, MD
Director of Medical Education and Clinical Innovation
Broward Health Medical Center
Fort Lauderdale, Florida
Author of the best selling book in cardiology:
Clinical Cardiology Made Ridiculously Simple

"Your book kept my interest all the way through. It was an excellent read, combining the wisdom of experts with your personal and professional experiences. Thank you for distilling the principles of achievement into such an instructional and motivating book."

Lee Sheldon, DMD
Founder
Institute for Dental Specialists
Melbourne, Florida

*"Thank you to Dr. Tom McCawley for an excellent, informative, and concise read in **A Blueprint for a Highly Successful Life: A Survival Guide for the Aftermath of the COVID-19 Pandemic.** This playbook has helped me to navigate this very trying time, both professionally and personally. Dr. McCawley's 5 Keys to a Highly Successful Life were a roadmap to follow to get my business through this tough time we are currently experiencing...and beyond! I am excited to use the information, and hopefully pass it on to my colleagues, friends and family to aid them. I cannot recommend this book enough to everyone, no matter what profession you are in, and no matter what stage of your career you are in - this will change your life!"*

William J. C. Roach, Au.D.
Ascent Audiology
Fort Lauderdale, Florida

"How successful could you be if you had virtually every obstruction to success removed—a blueprint, if you will, of how to navigate through a life that requires you to be a spouse, parent, business owner, professional, manager, employee, motivator and exceptional human being. Tom defines the term 'a man for others' better than any I have ever known. Tom goes to great efforts to translate his personal experiences into true learning opportunities to provide guidance in avoiding life's host of mistakes, or "messtakes," as he coins the term. Before I met Tom, I had as financially successful a practice as I could hope for, but I lacked balance, and was quickly approaching burnout. As a fantastic teacher, mentor and friend, Tom has helped me prioritize my life, and achieve the balance we all should seek to allow for a healthy and prosperous life. If you want a highly successful life, including financial peace of mind, read this book carefully, apply these lessons to your own life and pass them on to others."

Jason C. Stoner, DDS, MS
Columbus, Ohio

When I think of Tom McCawley, I am impressed by the balance he has created in his life and the multitude of people whom he has touched. Many aspects of this balance are evident in his most recent book. ***A Blueprint for a Highly Successful Life: A Survival Guide for the Aftermath of the COVID-19 Pandemic.***

"What is noteworthy is his willingness to relate his experiences, both *positive and challenging. In addition to being a world-class clinician and researcher, he has freely shared his wisdom with colleagues, and a generation of dental students, residents and dental hygienists. For me personally, he has been a most cherished friend. I have learned that when Tom makes a recommendation, I trust it implicitly, and like the Nike slogan, I 'Just do it!'"*

I. Stephen Brown, DDS, FACD, FICD
Professor of Periodontics
University of Pennsylvania School of Dental Medicine
Philadelphia, Pennsylvania

Preface

This book was inspired by the following quote, which I keep on my desk at my office:

"The final test of a leader is that he leaves behind him in others the conviction and the will to carry on."
— **Walter Lippmann**

This book is a synopsis of a lecture that my son, Mark, and I have given annually for four years to the junior dental students at Nova Southeastern School of Dental Medicine: A Blueprint for a Highly Successful Life! It also has excerpts from my previous book written in 2009, *"The 4 Simple Secrets to Avoiding Life's Big Financial Messtakes."*

Why a rewrite of my first book?
COVID-19!!

The COVID-19 disease caused by the coronavirus is not the only tragedy caused by this virus. The collateral damage to our spiritual, mental, physical, relationship and financial health is equally and, in some cases, more severe, and is the focus of this book. With the surge in COVID-19 infecting our friends, family members and co-workers, it's nearly impossible to avoid this collateral damage, which is causing us severe stress.

My first book on this subject was written after the 2008 financial crisis to throw a lifeline to people suffering from this financial meltdown. COVID-19 is an epic, likely even greater crisis, so I wanted to offer some help again with a shorter, easier to read synopsis of timeless information.

I suggest we return to basic proverbial principles to keep ourselves centered. *Avoiding 5 Big Messtakes* is one way to do this.

As M. Scott Peck says in the first sentence of his book, **The Road Less Traveled:** *"Life is difficult. Once we truly see this truth, we transcend it."*

He then adds: *"Life is a series of problems. How we respond to these problems determines the quality of our life."* He emphasizes that, *"Delaying gratification is the only decent way to live."*

This is THE road less traveled for many of us.

I use this principle daily to do the difficult things first so that I can enjoy the chance to play later. Work first, then play, helps prevent procrastination.

However, don't make the *mess*take that I have made many times by never getting around to play.

Remember the famous proverb about balancing both:

> **"All work and no play makes Jack a dull boy,**
> **but all play and no work makes Jack a mere toy."**

Do we want to complain about the COVID-19 crisis, or dig in, adapt, and turn this problem into an opportunity? The opportunity for me was the inspiration and time to write this book, and the impetus to make our office even safer.

In a sense, I feel like my mission is much like that of Jacob Marley's mission in Charles Dickens' beloved book, *A Christmas Carol*. When old miser Scrooge is visited by the ghost of his late partner, Jacob Marley, Marley warns Scrooge: "There is no amount of regret that can make amends for one's life's opportunity misused! Oh! Such was I!"

Scrooge argues: "But you were a good man of business, Jacob." "Business!," cries Marley. "Mankind was my business! The dealings of my trade were but a drop of water in the comprehensive ocean of my business! Hear me; I've come to warn you that you have yet a chance and hope of escaping this fate!"

Are you a Scrooge?
Will you heed Marley's warning?
Is mankind your business?

This book is primarily about avoiding the biggest *mess*take we could make — failing to integrate our pursuit of money into living a well-balanced, great life, even in exceedingly difficult times like now, because:

> **"Tough times never last but tough people do!"**
> **— Robert Schuller**

Because I have written this book from my perspective as a dentist, the principles in this book will be especially helpful for professionals and business owners.

My goal is to contribute to as many people as possible by changing the way we now commonly define success as primarily being rich and famous.

I propose a new definition of success that includes much more: encompassing spiritual, mental, physical, relationship and financial health. I call this living a highly successful life and finishing well.

> **"Get all the advice and instruction you can**
> **so that you can be wise the rest of your life."**
> **Proverbs 19:20**

It may sound like I have it all together in this book. I don't. I am a fellow traveler with you. These are just some bits of wisdom that I have picked up along the way to help improve my life, and hopefully yours.

It's also not some great discovery of mine. This is timeless wisdom from Solomon and others, for "there's nothing new under the sun."

> **"And there is nothing new under the sun.**
> **Is there anything of which it may be said, 'See, this is new?'**
> **No! It has already been said in ancient times before us."**
> **Ecclesiastes 1:10**

The main premise of this book is simply this:

I believe that Spiritual Health — a mission to make a positive difference in people's lives — is the key driving force for Living a Highly Successful Life. This is the critical **"WHY"** for doing almost everything, and my **"WHY"** for writing this book.

However, we can't make a difference if we are depressed, and our **Mental Health** is not good. This is "**THE WILL**" to make a difference.

We can't make a difference without good **Physical Health**. This gives us **"THE ENERGY."**

We can't make a difference with poor **Relationships**, because this is **"THE WAY"** that we contribute to others.

Finally, without good **Finances**, we don't have **"THE MEANS"** to make a difference.

We need excellence in all 5 Health's to live a Highly Successful Life, and survive the collateral damage of COVID-19 to these 5 Health's. The goal of this book is to help us to achieve this.

Decide for Yourself

Before I go further, I want to quote the words of the Dalai Lama to emphasize that:

> *"Although I speak from my own experience,*
> *I will not propose to you that my way is best.*
> *The decision is up to you!"*

Some have estimated that less than 50% of us reach the end of our life and <u>finish</u> well. Look around and you will notice that lots of people will end up broke, bitter, divorced, disabled, dead early, or some even disgraced. There are many paths to finishing well. But there are literally hundreds of ways to *MESS* up our lives and not finish well. Another goal of this book is to help us all avoid these *MESS*takes, and finish both long and well.

***"No one would begin
the building of a house
without first drafting a blueprint.
Why should your life
and its success
be any different?"***
— Stephen Covey
The Seven Habits of Highly Successful People

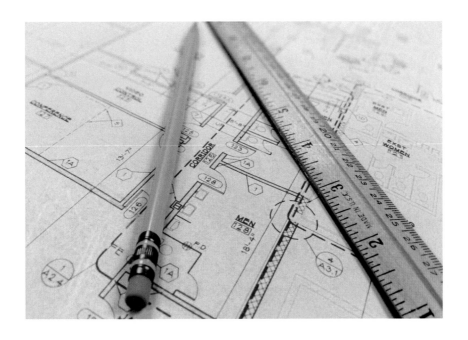

A Blueprint for A Highly Successful Life

1. Redefine Success!

2. Balance the Five Key Areas for a Highly Successful Life.

3. Avoid the Five Really Big *Mess*takes We Make!

4. Four Secrets to Financial Security.

5. Five Secrets to a Highly Successful Life!

Success - The attainment of wealth, fame, honors, or the like
***Random House Unabridged Dictionary*, 2020**

So, the common definition of success is being rich and famous. This is very short sighted. No mention of the several other areas of success that we will discuss below. I define success differently.

Going Beyond Success to Significance — My Definition of a Highly Successful Life is:

Going the extra mile to make
a positive difference in people's lives
through great relationships,
while feeling happy, satisfied, and peaceful,
healthy, energetic and financially free.
— Dr. Tom McCawley

It's relatively easy to write a definition of a highly successful life. The real question is: "How do you do it?" What are the simple secrets, the steps to achieving this? That's what this book is about.

Balance These Five Key Areas for a Highly Successful Life!

Spiritual Health

"The Mission"
"The Why!"

Mental Health

"The Will"

Physical Health

"The Energy"

Relationship Health

"The Way"

Financial Health

"The Means"

**With These Five Keys,
You Can Avoid Life's
Five Really Big *Mess*takes.**

Avoiding Life's Five "REALLY" BIG *Mess*takes

We Neglect to Do Our Best on Our 5 Healths

1. Spiritual: **We have no mission, so we live a life with no meaning, and don't make a positive difference in the lives of others.**

2. Mental: **We think we are a victim, being treated unfairly, or entitled, so we burn out, get depressed, and even sometimes, commit suicide.**

3. Physical: **We don't exercise, eat right, get regular medical checkups, or do the best we can to prevent contracting COVID-19 — which leads to lower energy, disability, and earlier death.**

4. Relationships: **We undervalue their importance and complain about them, resulting in divorce, infidelity, troubled kids, and few friends.**

5. Financial: **We overemphasize making money as an end in itself, and underemphasize managing and enjoying it wisely.**

Spiritual Health

The Mission!
"The Why!"

"When I say "spiritual,"
I do not necessarily
mean any kind of religious faith.
I mean having basic
good human qualities."

The Dalai Lama's Book of Wisdom

Are You Making a Positive Difference in the Lives of Others?

*"When you come to see your work
as a mission to help others —
you will never work a day in your life."*
— **Chuck Sorenson, PhD**

Our Office Mission:

*"Saving Lives
by Saving Smiles"*

Psychiatrist Victor Frankl, the author of ***Man's Search for Meaning***, said that:

> ### *"Those who have a why to live can bear with almost any how."*

He used his desire to write about his experiences that helped him survive, despite incredibly long odds, for three years in Nazi concentration camps.

My father used the same motivation to survive after being captured by the Germans in the Battle of the Bulge. He was placed in a closed railroad car for six days with little food and water. He survived by licking frozen water on the edge of the car. He then spent 99 days in a prison camp with little food, and went from 160 pounds to 100 pounds.

When he and his fellow soldiers were being marched to the rear, some of the soldiers would just give up, and were often shot. He was able to keep motivated and keep going because of a picture of my mother and myself which he carried with him. He would even show the picture to the guards in the camp, and they were sometimes nicer to him.

Thankfully, for my family and me, he had a "why" to live!

The photo which my dad carried during World War II to help give him the "why" to survive 99 days at Hitler's infamous Stalag IX-B.

The importance of mission cannot be overemphasized! It's what drove the writing of this book after seeing the distress caused by the coronavirus. I think about my mission every day and suggest you do the same.

What is your mission in all areas of your life? This will help you more than anything to survive the COVID-19 crisis.

"You don't have to do great things …
Just do small things with love."

"If you want to change the world,
go home and love your family."
— **Mother Teresa**

It's a BIG *Mess*take
to Neglect Our Spiritual Health —
Our Mission!

Mental Health

"The Will"

**"If you fail under pressure,
your strength is not very great."
Proverbs 24:10**

**"Learn to manage your mind,
or it will manage you."
— Tony Robbins**

**How Happy
and Peaceful
Are You?**

The following points summarize the basics of **Mental Health**, which is critical during the current COVID-19 crisis. They are what I've used now and throughout my life.

1. In her book, ***Burnout: The Cost of Caring,*** Christina Maslach says, "If all knowledge and advice about how to beat burnout could be summed up in one word, that word would be '**balance**.'" Her basic message is that giving of yourself must be balanced with giving *to* yourself. She urges us to practice "**detached concern**," which is a healthy blend of compassion and objectivity.

Realize that one will occasionally feel burnt-out. It's unavoidable for almost all of us. The key is to avoid making rash decisions when we are angry, tired or depressed. Rash decisions may cause us to crash and burn — like getting a divorce, quitting our job — or especially, in these high stress times, committing suicide, like a friend of mine did recently. You are not thinking rationally at this time. Know that, as Buddha said, "Nothing is permanent." Even COVID-19 will eventually pass. A treatment may be found, a vaccine has already been developed, or it will burn out like the Spanish flu did in 1920. Just stay as safe as possible until it does pass.

2. The next critical area is grit. 80% of life is just showing up by going out the door, which sometimes is the hardest part. Literally, hundreds of times I have not felt like going to work, but after I get there, I feel better almost every time. This has carried me through almost 10,000 days of work, with only one missed day from sickness. I just put one foot in front of the other. (My wife has helped keep my attendance record intact by locking the door after I walked out, and ignoring my pleas to let me back in!)

3. The next thing that helps me a lot is remembering Newton's laws of physics. Start and you will continue. Even more critical is the second law "In an isolated system, not taking on energy, entropy (degradation and disorder) always increases over time." **This is why things are always falling apart!** Like having a coronavirus crisis now.

As stated in the book, "***The Power of Bad***:"
• The world will always seem to be in crisis.
• The crisis is never as bad as it sounds.
• The solution could easily make things worse.

Think about the current COVID-19 crisis and other current crises. This is the latest of literally thousands of crises over the course of the history of mankind.

4. The fourth basic principle for **Mental Health** is writing down every day what you are grateful for. I go over this twice a day when I meditate, which also helps with **Mental Health** . It can be something as simple as being grateful for being born in the USA, and being alive and healthy. We won the lottery just by being born in this country. With all the trouble going on, I know what you're thinking, but look around at the other countries especially Africa and Asia.

These basic thoughts help me: **Turn lemons into lemonade, there is a silver lining in every cloud, and, there is an opportunity in every problem.** This sometimes takes me a few days to find, since it sometimes is not readily apparent. Regarding the coronavirus, the opportunity is in a global focus on creating a vaccine, which will likely result in better treatment for all viral diseases.

And **don't make a mountain out of a molehill.** Don't make things worse than they are. Keep things in perspective. This like thousands of crises before, will pass. Remember worse crises like the Spanish Flu, which lasted for two years and killed 30 million people, and World War II, which lasted for six years and killed 75 million people

Being resilient in tough times is vital to surviving and thriving in tough times like now. Physician therapist, Gail Gazelle describes how to do it in her just published book, *Everyday Resilience.*

She defines resilience as: "**A well of inner resources that allows you to weather the difficulties and challenges you encounter, without unnecessary mental, emotional, or physical stress**."

Sounds like just what we need right now! See her list of inner resources on the next page.

To enhance my resilience, I have been meditating for years. I recently discovered an enhanced guided meditation called SKY breath meditation-The Art of Living. It has helped quiet my mind, relieve some anxiety and helped me sleep better. Just do it! They suggest Five Keys to Happiness including: accepting people and situations as they are and don't see intention in other peoples mistakes and actions. Take the training to get the three other brilliant Keys. https://www.artofliving.org/us-en They also suggest doing two random acts of kindness each day to enhance the well-being of others and yourself.

The Six Habits of Highly Resilient People*

1. Resilient people remember that life is short. They recognize that the misfortunes of life happen to everyone, including themselves – and they react with strength, compassion, and wisdom when they do. **[They realize that my mother was right when she told me: "Time heals all wounds."]**

2. Resilient people let go of perfectionism. They recognize that perfection is unattainable – and realize that doing their best is the way to go.

3. Resilient people lean into gratitude. They spend time appreciating what they have, and try not to focus on what they don't. **[When I am feeling a little down, I make a list of all the things that I am grateful for. It works almost every time.]**

4. Resilient people know which thoughts to believe. They recognize which thought patterns are serving them, and which aren't. **[Especially beware of the temptation to think yourself unfairly treated, a victim, or entitled.]**

5. Resilient people let go of what they can't control. They ask themselves: Is this something I can change? If yes, they think about how best to intervene. If no, they remind themselves that the thing they always have control over is themselves.

6. Resilient people have a growth mindset. In order to weather the difficulties in our work, we have to believe that we can shift our own behaviors, improve, and grow. **[Like applying some of the ideas in this book.]**

I read this list whenever I have a problem, which is almost every day. It helps a lot. Try it.

(Based on an article by Gail Gazelle, M.D., author of **Everyday Resilience: A Practical Guide to Build Inner Strength and Weather Life's Challenges.)*

Banishing Burnout
Leiter and Maslach

Burnout is lost energy, lost enthusiasm, and lost confidence.
Burnout is the biggest occupational hazard of the 21st century.
How does one avoid **Burnout**? **You Can't!**
Therefore, when you are fatigued, in a low mood, or angry,
don't make any rash decisions and

CRASH AND BURN!

"Second thoughts are ever wiser."
— Euripides

Persistence/Grit

- **80% of success is just showing up.**
- **You're never beaten if you don't quit.**
- **Put one foot in front of the other!**
- **Fall down eight, get up nine.**
- **A steady pace wins the race.**

"Nothing in the world can take the place of persistence.
Talent will not; nothing is more common than
*   unsuccessful men with talent.*
Persistence and determination alone are omnipotent.
The slogan Press On! has solved, and always will solve,
*   the problems of the human race."*
— Calvin Coolidge

(even COVID-**19**?)

Newton's Laws of Physics [and Success]

"An object in motion will remain in motion
unless acted on by a larger force."
Start, you'll continue!

"In an isolated system, not taking on energy, entropy –
degradation and disorder – always increases over time."
This is why things are always falling apart!
Keep going or you go backwards!

Thanks!

How the New Science of Gratitude
Can Make You Happier
Robert A. Emmons, Ph.D.

"Those that live with a
*sense of gratitude **and cultivate***
their gratitude each day
by writing down
what they are grateful for
enjoy 25% greater happiness."

I write down what I am grateful for each night,
and it really helps me be happier.

Just do it!

In times of crisis like COVID-19, it's good to be reminded to keep our heads about us, as Rudyard Kipling suggests in his famous poem "If:"

"If you can keep your head about you
When all about you are losing theirs, and blaming it on you.
If you can trust yourself when all men doubt you,
But make allowance for their doubting too,
If you can meet with Triumph and Disaster
And treat those two impostors just the same;
If you can force your heart and nerve and sinew
To serve your turn long after they are gone,
And so hold on when there is nothing in you
Except the Will which says to them: 'Hold on!'
If neither foes nor loving friends can hurt you,
If all men count with you, but none too much;
If you can fill the unforgiving minute
With sixty seconds' worth of distance run,
Yours is the Earth and everything that's in it,
And — which is more — you'll be a Man, my son!

It's a BIG *Mess*take to Neglect Our Mental Health!

Physical Health

"The Energy"

How can you improve your health?

**Physical Health Comes Before
Fiscal Health. It's the Only Real Problem!**

Being Dead is Bad for Business

"You Should Be Dead!"

"A wise person thinks much about death,
while the fool thinks only
about having a good time now."
Ecclesiastes 7:4

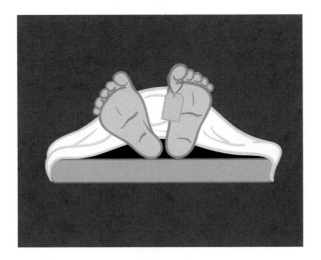

I opened my eyes in the hospital room to find my wife, Brenda, standing over me after what I thought was an unnecessary angiogram.

"You should be dead!" she said.

I had just dodged becoming another statistic of a surprising sudden death, like the late host of NBC's, Meet the Press, Tim Russert.

I, too, had a major blockage in "the widow maker," the left anterior descending coronary artery.

Dr. Michael Chizner, my cardiologist, said, that with a 95% blockage, it was doubtful I would have made it through the weekend.

I had suffered an acute plaque rupture of a major coronary artery. This would have led to certain death without Dr. Chizner's insightful diagnosis, and skillful intervention to open my blocked artery with a stent.

Like most people do, I had ignored my symptoms of fatigue, and a dull pain below my sternum. Don't make this big *mess*take!

It was almost my fatal *Mess*take! I ignored symptoms of indigestion, fatigue, and dizziness when exercising. Three months earlier, I had had a perfect physical exam.

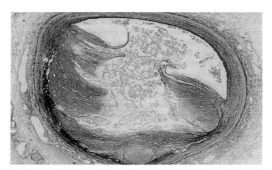

Acute plaque rupture from center of plaque

This happened to me 12 years ago after climbing the Great Wall of China. Fortunately, I had only 95% blockage of the "Widow Maker" heart artery, and made it home to get a stent before it blocked entirely.

What I Didn't Know —
Almost a Fatal *Mess*take!

1. A heart attack is not usually a sharp pain over the heart.

2. 50% of heart attacks occur in people with no risk factors.

3. 70% occur when a smaller plaque ruptures.

4. EMS (Emergency Medical Services) takes 10 minutes to arrive, and patients have only a 5% survival rate!

5. Therefore, <u>we</u> must use an AED (automated external defibrillator) within 5 minutes or less to save a life!

6. Angioplasty (clearing the artery) within 90 minutes will greatly reduce heart damage!

So Don't Delay Going to the Hospital!

A Healthy Lifestyle Can Add 14 Years to Your life!

A study in the ***Archives of Internal Medicine***, Jan. 28, 2008, which followed 20,244 people for 11 years, concluded:

A healthy fat diet, (no trans or saturated fats), exercise, weight control, not smoking, and controlling your blood pressure can add 14 years to your life!

How to Protect Against COVID-19

A disease caused by a new coronavirus — severe acute respiratory syndrome coronavirus 2 (SARS-CoV-2) — likely coming from bats

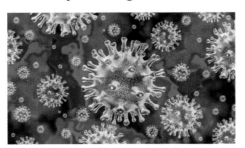

Wear a mask in public, wash your hands frequently, and avoid touching your mouth, nose or eyes.

Avoid the Three Cs: Closed Spaces, Crowded Places, and Close-Contact Settings.

- Closed Spaces. Avoid closed spaces with poor ventilation that could allow contagious droplets to linger in the air.

- Crowded Places. Avoid crowded places with many people nearby; the greater the number of individuals in an area, the greater the chances of COVID-19 spreading from person-to-person.

- Close-Contact Settings. Avoid close-range conversations and stay at least six feet from others.

Gum Disease: "It Can Kill You!" And Make COVID-19 Worse

American comedian Soupy Sales once said, "Be true to your teeth and they won't be false to you." As a specialist treating gum diseases, I would be remiss if I did not mention that the bacteria infecting the gums can affect your health by spreading to the heart and other organs. The August 2020 issue of the *Journal of Neurology* reported that dementia was linked to periodontal disease in a large group of 8,300 people followed for 20 years.

Evidence is mounting that periodontal disease can also increase your susceptibility to COVID-19, and greatly increase the risk of death from this virus.

We have pioneered identifying and treating these bacteria linked to the inflammation associated with many systemic diseases, and now COVID-19. We use the microscope, and sometimes culture, to identify the actual cause of the periodontal infection.

Instead of treating just the resultant pockets, we focus on treating and curing the bacterial cause. This results in better long term outcomes, and less recurrence of the infection.

To prevent gum disease and protect your health, we recommend regular professional cleanings, and **The FBI,** to control plaque. The **FBI** includes these four steps in order: **T**ongue cleaning, **F**lossing, **B**rushing, and **I**rrigating with a diluted antiseptic mouthwash.

For more advanced problems, there is a breakthrough in treatment, which I helped pioneer, using a new, specially-designed Nd:YAG laser.

Like LASIK for eye surgery, minimally-invasive laser surgery can now replace the blade and sutures for treating most forms of infectious, inflammatory gum disease by more predictably killing the bacteria and regrowing your bone, saving your smile, and possibly your life.

Our goal is to offer patients therapies that we would want for ourselves. We have literally searched the world for the most gentle and effective treatments. This has led us to minimally invasive treatments that combine accurate diagnosis of the causes of periodontal and implant infections with proven laser, antibiotic, antiseptic and occlusal therapies to provide more predictable, long-lasting treatment often to, in many cases, cure, not just control, periodontal infections.

To learn much more information about oral health see my and my son, Mark's, book, *"Saving Your Teeth, Implants and Your Health"* downloadable on our website **mccawley.com,** or available on Amazon.

Say Good Night to Insomnia

In his book, ***Say Good Night to Insomonia***, Gregg Jacobs, Ph.D., says:

It's important to go to bed and, especially, get up at the same time every day, including weekends, to maintain our sleep cycle.

Sleeping in a cool room greatly aids sleep.

It is normal to sleep less, and more lightly, as we age.

Many people don't need 8 hours of sleep; 5 1/2 hours of core sleep is enough.

Worrying about insomnia will hurt you more than insomnia.

Dozing is almost as good. You are still getting rest.

A poor night's sleep does not produce significant adverse effects on the next day's performance, except on monotonous tasks.

Sleeping pills do not treat the causes of insomnia.

Too much sleep can make you lethargic.

A 45-minute nap before 4 pm is good.

Exercising before 7 pm to make yourself physically tired will help you sleep better.

Getting proper rest is important to mental and physical health. This is the best book on sleep that I have found.

*"We spend our health building our wealth,
then we desperately spend our wealth
to hang on to our remaining health."*
— **Robert Kiyosaki**
Rich Dad, Poor Dad

**It's a BIG, Maybe Fatal *Mess*take,
Not To Do Everything Possible
To Protect Ourselves From the Coronavirus,
And Not to Take Great Care
of Our Physical Health!**

Relationship Health

"The Way"

"Overlooking another person's faults preserves love."
Proverbs 17:9

I will remember that we are all connected, so that I choose to love people despite the reasons they give me not to love them, and ignore and forgive their bad behavior, because I understand them as suffering and looking for love, as we all are, including me.

"Kind words are like honey sweet to the soul and healthy for the body."
Proverbs 16:24

I will then proactively fill their buckets with random acts of kindness, love and positive recognition. This statement also applies to how we treat ourselves, since we can be our own worst critic. I believe the quality of our lives is directly proportional to the quality of our **Relationships** with family, friends, co-workers, and clients.

The Real Purpose of
All Relationships?
To Magnify
Our Experience of Life!

— **Tony Robbins**
Get the Edge
Day 3

Wall Street Journal, August 5, 2020

"Even in the best of times, marriage and Relationships are hard work. But the pandemic has produced a pressure cooker inside homes, straining even strong partnerships and, experts say, likely breaking others.

Families are cooped up, with spouses trying to work while also taking care of their kids. Job losses, caring for at-risk elderly parents, arguments over what's safe, and disagreements over school reopening are all taking a toll.

'Where there was a crack, there is now a rupture,' says Kathryn Smerling, a family therapist in New York City."

How to Handle COVID Stress
In Relationships

1. Keep in mind that this is a unique situation.

2. Think twice about big Relationship decisions during this time.

3. Don't forget to play.

B egun in 1938, the Harvard Grant Study of Adult Development charted the physical and emotional health of over 200 men, for 75 years, starting with their undergraduate days in college.

**<u>Great Relationships were the primary determinates for
life satisfaction, happiness, and a longer life.</u>**

Being a genius is no guarantee of Relationship ability. Albert Einstein and Stephan Hawking both had IQs of 160, and were clueless about Relationships with their wives.

"Who can find a virtuous wife?
For her worth is far above rubies.
She does him good and not evil
all the days of her life."
Proverbs 31:10, 12

The Man's Guide to Women
— John Gottman

Choose a Partner Carefully!

"**Your Relationship will cause you 90% of the joy or sorrow in your life.** Avoid deciding in infatuation"

"A great Relationship is a mix of heart (kindness), mind (mental health), and body (sexual chemistry). You need all three!"

"Avoid victims, princesses [princes], drama queens [kings], and competitors."

The Seven Principles for Making Marriage Work
— John Gottman

41% of marriages end in divorce-why?

1. Criticism: 5-1 positive feedback in good marriages vs. 0.8 – 1 in bad marriages

> *"It is better to live alone in the desert than with a crabby, complaining wife [or husband]."*
> **Proverbs 21:20**

2. Contempt: The spouse is inferior. This is the worst!

3. Stonewalling: More common in males, who go into a cave.

4. Defensiveness: Refusing to accept influence from partner.

John Gottman and his wife, Julie, have done the definitive research on Relationships. My wife Brenda and I have attended their two-day course in Seattle twice. (I flunked it the first time!) Invaluable, and we recently celebrated 40 years of marriage.

Their most recent book, ***Eight Dates - Essential Conversations for a Lifetime of Love,*** is also very valuable. Brenda and I have gone through this book twice. As they emphasize, "happily ever after" is not by chance. It's by choice.

Tierney and Baumeister, 2019

Bad things have a much more potent effect than good deeds on us and others. It takes at least four good deeds to overcome one bad deed.

Practice the negative golden rule: Don't do unto others anything that they don't like.

This great book changed the way that I interact with people to focus more on not doing things that irritate my wife and others.

"Parenting is possibly the most important job on the planet!"

Some of My Parenting Suggestions to Help Raise Smart and Successful Kids

1. Marry a smart, mentally-healthy spouse. Genetics is important. (See Gottman, top of page 26)

2. Take total responsibility for their education and values beginning when they are babies.

3. Teach them to be polite and courteous, and know right from wrong.

4. Teach them at home, and also send them to school primarily for socialization.

5. Don't blame their teachers if they are not doing well.

6. Have high expectations and keep a close eye on them.

7. Give them space with clear boundaries.

8. Help them learn that the world does not owe them a living.

*"Many men
can build a fortune,
but very few
can build a family."*
— **J. S. Bryan**

*My 75th birthday - 4 sons, 7 grandchildren,
2 daughters-in-law*

Financial Health

"The Means"

**The Biggest Financial *MESS*take
We Make:**

**Focusing too much time and energy
on making money,
and not enough on
managing and spending it
in a way that adds value
to our life and others.**

*" We have seen too many ruin their lives
by placing too much time and energy
into materialistic pursuits while
neglecting the things that matter most."*
— Peter Dawson
The Better Way

How Financially Secure Are You?

4 Simple Secrets To Financial Security

Over 90% of Dentists Can't Afford to Retire.
Greg Stanley, Dental Consultant
September 2020

"Because of the pandemic, the average age that a dentist can afford to retire is projected to be 74."
Roger Levin, DDS, Dental Consultant
October, 2020

More than half of millennials surveyed feel overwhelmed by Financial obligations, compared with 39% of Gen Xers, and even 31% of boomers who are nearing retirement.
Sardone - Wall Street Journal
March 13, 2020

1. **Earn!**
   Maximize your earning potential and net income.

2. **Save!**
   Don't spend it all.
   Pay yourself first from the beginning.
   Start at 3 to 20% of your net income to get in the habit.
   Save 15 times your net income for retirement to give yourself alternatives to working at age 60.

3. **Don't lose!**
   Diversify to get rich slowly, stay married, and get insurance to protect yourself.
   If you lose 50%, you need to get 100% return to recover.

4. **Enjoy!**
   Spend it wisely on things that add value to your life and the lives of others, like family, travel, personal development, reasonable homes, hobbies and helping others, i.e. pro bono or reduced fee work.

If It Sounds Too Good to Be True...It Is!

The *Forbes* journalist, William Barrett, outlines seven *mess*takes we investors make. This is a wonderful opportunity to learn not only from the *mess*takes of others, but from our own, which is often the very best way to learn! I've added my personal comments to his terrific list.

1. The Reputation Ruse – counting on the person's reputation when we make an investment, instead of checking it out closely. After all, Madoff was a former chairman of the board of directors for the NASDAQ. He should have read Solomon's Proverbs. It might have helped him.

> *"It is better to be poor and honest*
> *than rich and crooked"*
> **Proverbs 28:6**

2. The Affinity Fraud – believing that because somebody is a member of our church or club, or is a friend, they can therefore be trusted with our money. This was part of Bernie Madoff's scheme. He surely could be trusted not to steal money from friends, from his club, and synagogue, couldn't he?

To this list, I would also add family members. It is not uncommon for people to lose a lot of money investing with family members. Although it can be fraud, it is more often simply poor investing. But the money is lost, nonetheless.

3. Falling for a Free Lunch – falling for claims that are too good to be true. Madoff's genius was offering very good returns regularly, but not extraordinary returns.

In the words of Solomon:

> *"A greedy person tries to get rich quick,*
> *but it only leads to poverty."*
> **Proverbs 28:22**

4. Trusting Regulators to Protect Us – The Securities and Exchange Commission (SEC) rarely discovers things until after the fact. Henry Markopolos wrote five different letters to the SEC from 1999 to 2006 pointing out problems with the Madoff investment scheme, with minimal response.

To this I would add, trusting our associations and organizations to protect us. They often receive large kickbacks for recommending investment programs and insurance. These need to be investigated just like any other investment. As a dentist, I had to find a place for the following advice from Solomon. I think it works well here.

> *"Putting confidence in an unreliable person*
> *is like chewing with a toothache."*
> **Proverbs 25:19**

5. Putting All Our Eggs in One Basket – It pays to diversify for safety. This is critical. In my defense, I think I would only have put part of my money with Madoff.

> *"Divide your portion into seven, or even to eight,*
> *for you do not know what misfortune may occur."*
> **Ecclesiastes 11:2**

Like the COVID-19 pandemic!

6. Falling for an Exclusive and Secretive Investment Idea –
If it's so good, why do they need our money? I'm still pretty upset that no one invited me to invest with Madoff. But I do feel better remembering Groucho Marx's words: "I refuse to join any club that would want me as a member anyway."

7. Fox Guarding the Henhouse –

No third-party auditing of the results. Be **very careful** that all your investments are being watched over by competent and **honest** third parties.

Be especially watchful of all commission based salesmen. Don't completely trust anybody. Keep in mind the Madoff, Enron and, in Ft. Lauderdale, Rothstein scandals.

There is another scandal happening someplace right now.

Will you be part of it?

How We Lose Money!

1. Gambling and Greed — Casinos, risky investments. I know of someone who lost over $600,000 at the Hard Rock Casino! Mark Twain summed all this up well when he said,

> *"There are two times in a man's life*
> *when he should not speculate:*
> *when he can't afford it, and when he can."*

Sadly, he knew very well what he was talking about – he went bankrupt investing in new inventions for printing, which made him bitter at the end of his life. Unfortunately, he did not finish well.

2. Brokers, tax shelters, bankers — I don't recommend individual stocks, because you must make two decisions correctly on when to buy and when to sell. In addition, I believe your time is best used maximizing your earnings in your own job or profession. If you use a stockbroker frequently, you'll likely end up "broker." They make money only through commissions made trading. One of their jobs is to sell you the product their company is currently pushing, which often has a higher commission than other products. The analysts for these brokerage firms are often simply touts for the stocks they are promoting, and seldom have the courage to issue sell recommendations. They should be ignored completely. They have too much conflict of interest.

**They see us
as a
money tree
to be picked!**

In the same vein, famous investor Bernard Baruch said, "Never pay the slightest attention to what a company president says about his stock." Obviously, company presidents have the same conflict of interest as their analysts.

> ***"Only simpletons believe everything they are told!***
> ***The prudent carefully consider their steps."***
> **Proverbs 14:15**

3. Consumptive lifestyle — Expensive houses which leave us house poor; expensive cars; expensive equipment; expensive educations for us and our children, which leave us education poor; living the high life on a **hedonic treadmill**, wanting more and more to be happy.

> ***"Even if you win the rat race, you're still a rat!"***
> **— Lily Tomlin**

4. Divorce: "You Can't Be Serious!" — My initial thought was "You can't be serious!," (the famous statement by tennis great John McEnroe) when my first wife returned from her high school reunion, and told me that she was leaving me that night. Hardly believing my ears, I said, "We have three children, ages two, four and six, and you want to leave tonight?" I asked her if she could give me a day, so that at the very least, I could get some help to watch the kids. She agreed, and left the following day.

As you might imagine, this was a difficult time for me. It led to my first significant depression. I got through it with the help of housekeepers, friends, family, psychologists, and grit – putting one foot in front of the other. The opportunity in this big problem is that I am much closer to my boys, having been a solo parent for seven years. And I found a terrific new wife, life partner of 40 years, and great mother for the boys.

My three sons —
just before
my first wife left

By getting divorced, we can often lose much of our net worth, and suffer considerable emotional pain. Despite my best efforts to put it back together, my Relationship with my first wife was essentially unsalvageable. I definitely don't recommend staying in a truly bad relationship just for the money. Just be sure that you have done everything possible to save the relationship, and understand the Financial consequences of a breakup.

A study by Jay Zagorsky in the ***Journal of Sociology*** reported on the financial status of 9,055 people from 1985 to 2000. Those who divorce lose, on average, three fourths of their personal net worth. I have a dentist friend whose divorce cost him $3.2 million after taxes.

These stories have led to a new definition for stock split – when your ex-spouse and their lawyer split your assets equally between themselves.

Financial **Wisdom**

If something can't go on forever, it won't!
As in Aesop's fable, be an ant not a grasshopper
and save for the inevitable winter,
like the COVID-19 pandemic now.

Stocks and home prices go up and down!

Return of principal is more important
than return on principal.

Save early!
Water the tree before you pick the fruit.

**Think of your dollars as freedom
fighters to give you choices!**

**Whatever you do,
don't kill the goose
that lays the golden egg—
your earning potential!
This is the best source of money,
not investing.**

Financial Freedom Blueprint

Dr. Ace's Guide to Personal and Financial Freedom

Dr. Albert "Ace" Goerig

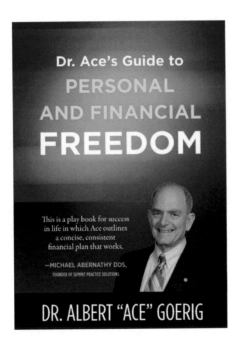

"The Great American Scam consists of monthly debt payments, which has changed the American Dream into a nightmare."

"If you live big taking on more debt, you will give to creditors up to 2/3 of your life's earnings in interest."

I consider this one of the best books ever written on finances for professionals. Just get it!

If he looks like a millionaire, he's not!

In Texas they say,
"Big Hat, No Cattle!"

Be balance sheet wealthy,
not appearance wealthy

"Know when enough is enough,
and that better doesn't always mean more."
— **Peter Dawson**
A Better Way

But What About The COVID-19 Economic Fallout?

"It was the best of times, it was the worst of times, it was the age of wisdom, it was the age of foolishness, it was the spring of hope, it was the winter of despair."

So begins Charles Dickens' *A Tale of Two Cities*, a fascinating epic written in 1859, which is worth contemplating today. Which is it? How we really see our circumstances is our choice isn't it?

Some would say this all sounds good on paper, but what about the REALLY tough times we're facing today?

Financial intelligence is never more important than in tough times! In good times, almost anything works. We wouldn't be human if we weren't concerned about what's going on economically. We are definitely facing some Financially difficult times.

However, tough times never last, but tough people do. Again, things can't go on forever.

Remember that our parents and grandparents survived The Great Depression, which essentially lasted for 12 years, from 1929 to the beginning of the Second World War in 1941. The Dow Jones Industrial Average dropped 89%, and did not recover to the pre-1929 levels until November 23, 1954. Almost half of all homes went into foreclosure, and unemployment reached 25%, with no unemployment insurance available.

That generation also lived through several of the worst wars in history. My father was captured by the Germans in the Battle of the Bulge, and spent six days being transported in a train car with little food or water. Our parents and grandparents survived these hard times pretty well, and so will we.

If we compare ourselves to those in most other countries, we are in considerably better shape. Ask yourself, where would you like to go that's better?

In the book, *Super Freakonomics*, the authors point out that: "It is a fact of life that people love to complain, particularly about how terrible the modern world is compared with the past. They are nearly always wrong. On just about any dimension you can think of – warfare, crime, income, education, transportation, worker safety, health – the 21st century is far more hospitable to the average human than any earlier time. For one example, consider deaths in childbirth. Just 100 years ago, the rate was more than 50 times higher."

For much more detail on **Financial** health,
see my previous book,
which is available on Amazon.

The 4 Simple Secrets to Avoiding Life's BIG Financial MESStakes

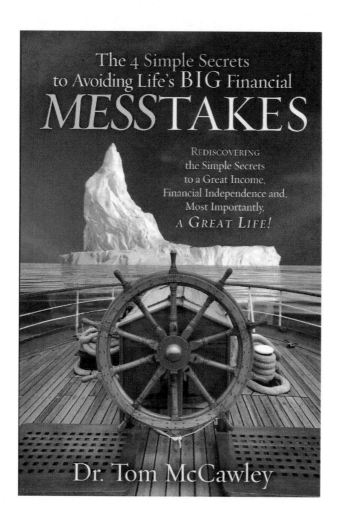

Enjoy Your Money Wisely!

"Just living isn't enough," said the butterfly,
"one must also have freedom, sunshine
and a little flower."
— Hans Christian Anderson

In his book, **The Better Way**, the late great Dr. Peter Dawson says that this principle changed his life. "**The either/or rule:** Every decision involving time keeps me from devoting that time to something else. So I must ask if what I am spending my time on is more important than what I could be doing in the same amount of time."

Let's use this principle. It may change our lives too.

Money spent wisely can give you the freedom to pursue your passions, your mission and your health, and it can buy you time with friends and family, all of which will increase your happiness.

Spend your money and your time on things that support your happiness – experiences, relationships, family, health, hobbies and helping others.

Understanding Money and Happiness

Money is something we choose to trade our life energy for: it can be a terrific servant or a tyrannical master.

> *"Happy is the person who finds wisdom and gains understanding. For the profit of wisdom is better than silver, and her wages are better than gold."*
> **Proverbs 3:13**

There is considerable evidence that money, at least beyond a certain amount, doesn't buy much additional happiness. The Harvard psychology professor, Daniel Gilbert, talks about this in his book, **Stumbling on Happiness.** He points out: "It hurts to be hungry, cold and scared, but once you have bought your way out of these burdens, the rest of your money is an increasingly useless pile of paper."

Jason Zweig, in his intriguing book, *Your Money and Your Brain*, says that one of the great discoveries of neuroeconomics is that expectation is more intense than experience. The thought of getting rich or hitting the jackpot is more pleasant for many people than the reality of getting rich or hitting the jackpot. This is the central reason why so many people were unhappy, even when they had unbelievable affluence before the COVID-19 crisis. Unfortunately, many of us don't learn from this *mess*take.

Charles Dickens dispenses this advice on money and happiness in his mostly autobiographical book, *David Copperfield*. His character, Mr. Micawber, who ends up in debtor's prison, bemoans: "Annual income twenty pounds, annual expenditure nineteen, nineteen six, result: happiness. Annual income twenty pounds, annual expenditure twenty pounds, ought and six, result: misery."

Dickens knew well what he was talking about. His father was sent to debtors' prison when Charles was 12 years old, forcing Charles to work long hours in miserable conditions to help pay off the family debt. His personal experience as a child laborer inspired some of his other books, including Oliver Twist.

A more recent lesson comes from billionaire Zappos.com Inc. co-founder Tony Hsieh, who died in a November, 2020 house fire, likely while playing with fire. Hsieh's death was the culmination of a more than six-month downward spiral into alcohol and drugs after selling Zappos to Amazon for more than one billion dollars. Hsieh, who brought online shoe-shopping to the masses, ironically, wrote a bestselling book on company culture, "Delivering Happiness."

Are You Rich or Wealthy?

In his just published book, ***The Psychology of Money: Timeless Lessons on Wealth, Greed, and Happiness***, Morgan Housel talks about the difference.

Mr. Housel urges investors to think about what money and wealth are for. He draws a critical distinction between being rich (having a high current income), and being wealthy (having the freedom to choose not to spend money).

Many rich people aren't wealthy, Mr. Housel argues, because they feel the need to spend a lot of money to show others how rich they are. **He defines the optimal savings level as "the gap between your ego and your income."** Wealth consists in caring less about what others think about you, and more about using your money to control how you spend your time.

He writes: **"The ability to do what you want, when you want, with who[m] you want, for as long as you want to, pays the highest dividend that exists in finance."**

Three Simple Secrets to Financial Security

1. The confidence that we have the ability to figure out for ourselves how to make more money than we spend, or spend less than we make.

2. Be grateful for and make the best of however much or little money we have.

3. Don't participate in the money myth: the belief that we can accurately predict what is going to happen, and therefore bet on the future ratio of buyers to sellers.

In my own life, I have invested in extensive travel with my wife and my family. During the past 25 years, my wife and I have visited all seven continents, 85 countries, and the north and south polar regions twice each. We have taken the family along on many of our trips. These trips have created great memories for all our family, which are priceless experiences.

Botswana and Victoria Falls, July 2019
16 family members — priceless!

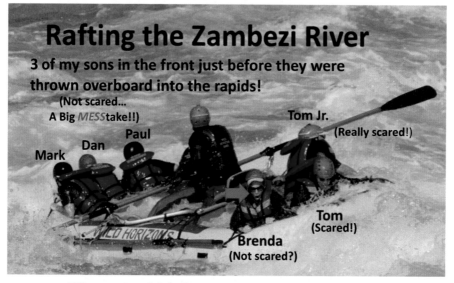

The second highest-rated rapid in the world!
Fortunately the crocodiles stayed on shore...
or maybe they weren't hungry?

For another example of investing in experiences, on a trip to Rwanda, I climbed to 10,000 feet near the top of a volcano to see the mountain gorillas. There are only about 400 of them left in the world, and none in captivity.

It is a spectacular sight to come across a troop of 25 mountain gorillas feeding in a high-altitude rain forest.

The climb was very difficult, but worth the effort. After watching for a while, I began photographing a young male silverback. When I asked the guide, "Is this the aggressive one?" he answered, "Yes!" A moment later, the 425-pound male silverback gorilla charged me.

I assumed it was either a fake charge, or that he would turn to the side.

Wrong! He ran right over the top of me!

Fortunately, we were in almost waist high brush, and I fell backwards into it. The sun was blocked out for an instant. I felt just two medium hard thumps on my chest.

Physically, I wasn't harmed. But momentarily, my psyche was severely damaged.

Our driver said he had been coming to this area for over 20 years and never known this to happen.

It certainly created a memory (maybe a nightmare?) for me that is priceless now that I'm back home alive, and several years have passed.

**This 425-pound mountain gorilla charged
and ran over the top of me,
creating a great memory (nightmare?)
for my family and me.**

Five Keys to a Highly Successful Life!

Spiritual Health

"The Mission"
"The Why!"

Mental Health

"The Will"

Physical Health

"The Energy"

Relationship Health

"The Way"

Financial Health

"The Means"

**What Are the
Five Great Secrets to a
Highly Successful Life?**

The Five GREAT SECRETS to Avoiding Life's BIG *MESS*takes And Living A Highly Successful Life!

Do Your Best to Enjoy Each Day And Make it Great!

Carpe Diem!

1. Spiritual: **Make a positive difference in other people's lives by going the extra mile to make your help helpful, creating all the happiness you can, and relieving all the misery you can.**

2. Mental: **Remember to choose your thoughts to avoid being a victim, to <u>expect</u> problems, and turn them into opportunities.**

3. Physical: **Exercise regularly, eat less calories than you burn, get adequate rest, regular medical checkups, and do your best to prevent contracting COVID-19.**

4. Relationships: **Love people, overlook their faults, then fill their buckets with recognition and acts of kindness.**

5. Financial: **Spend less than you make, or make more than you spend, don't lose it — then enjoy it wisely.**

*"Better is a handful with quietness,
than both hands full with travail
and vexation of the spirit."*
Ecclesiastes 4:6

*"For what it's worth:
It's never too late to be
whoever you want to be."*
— F. Scott Fitzgerald

The End

Epilogue: Pass It On

I hope your review of my book will be better than the one comedian Groucho Marx wrote for S. J. Perelman's book, *Monkey Business*: "From the moment I picked up your book until I laid it down, I was convulsed with laughter. Someday I intend reading it."

The Beginning...

Congratulations on making it to the end of this book. Hopefully, you are now at the beginning of a new more helpful, happier, healthier, wealthier, and wiser financial and personal life. Thank you for sharing my quest to live a highly successful life. I learned a lot along the way.

Since word of mouth is the best advertisement, if you found this book helpful, and you feel comfortable doing so, please pass it on to as many people as possible, and write a review of it on Amazon.

It's purpose is to make the biggest possible contribution to the most people, by leaving a legacy of joy and hope for present and future generations as they manage present crises like the COVID-19 pandemic, and any future crises which follow.

Wishing you a highly successful and healthy life,

About the Author

Dr. Tom McCawley earned his dental degree from the University of Illinois College of Dentistry, and a Certificate of Advanced Graduate Study in Periodontics from the Boston University School of Graduate Dentistry.

From 1969 to 1972, he served in the U.S. Army as Chief of Periodontics at the Baumholder, Germany Dental Center.

He has practiced periodontics in Fort Lauderdale since 1972. He is past president of the Florida Academy of Dental Practice Administration, and the Florida Association of Periodontists.

He is a Fellow of the American College of Dentists, has been a member of the Board of Directors of the North American Society of Periodontists since 1990, and a visiting lecturer at Nova Southeastern University (NSU) College of Dental Medicine since 1997.

Dr. McCawley has studied and lectured on life management, financial management, and dental practice management for over 40 years. He has lectured more than 200 times on these subjects, including at the University of Southern California, the University of Florida, and the NSU College of Dental Medicine, as well as to local and state dental groups.

After the financial crisis in 2009, he wrote his first book, ***The Four Simple Secrets to Avoiding Life's Big Financial Messtakes***. Some of the material in this book is taken from this previous book.

He has co-written two other books with his son, Mark: ***Saving Your Teeth, Implants and Your Health*** and ***Diagnosing and Treating Oral Diseases and Orofacial Pain.***

These books are all available on Amazon and on his website, mccawley.com.

• He presents his ***"Blueprint for a Highly Successful Life!"*** material in lectures annually to the dental students at NSU, and much of this book is taken from this lecture.

• Dr. McCawley was honored to be appointed to the Florida State Board of Dentistry to help protect the health and welfare of the public from dental treatments which do not meet the standard of care, and also to help elevate and maintain the professional standards of dentistry in Florida.

• He lectures annually to the periodontal graduate students at NSU on another of his interests, microbiology, and the use of antibiotics to treat periodontal disease. He recently received an award from the university for more than 20 years of outstanding contributions to the periodontal department.

• Dr. McCawley is one of the pioneers in using lasers to treat periodontal disease. He had the first Nd:YAG laser in the country in 1990. He has personally treated over 5,000 patients with laser technology, and lectures frequently on new minimally-invasive, breakthrough laser treatments for periodontal disease.

• He has published numerous articles in dental journals and newsletters, and is co-editor of a dental newsletter, ***The PerioDontaLetter***, which mails to approximately 5,000 dentists.

• He received the Gold Medal Award from Millennium Laser for his pioneering research that demonstrated that the Laser Assisted New Attachment procedure killed all the bacteria in periodontal pockets almost every time. **(See photo on page 55.)**

Dr. McCawley challenges and grades himself at the end of each day to avoid life's five really big *mess*takes, and to live fully in each of the five key areas he defines as essential to living a highly successful life – Spiritually by making the biggest possible contribution to others, **Mentally** by taking responsibility for a positive attitude, **Physically** by staying in peak physical health and shape, by creating great **Relationships**, and finally by building Financial freedom, which enables him to contribute to others and fully enjoy his life.

He has been happily married to Brenda for 40 years, and has four sons. Three of his sons are lawyers, and one is a periodontist who practices with him. He has seven grandchildren. All his children and grandchildren live in Fort Lauderdale.

His hobbies are his family, practicing periodontics with his "Dream Team,"— **(see photo on page 55)** — tennis, fitness, travel, and writing, lecturing, and researching about periodontics, and especially, living, writing, and lecturing about living a highly successful life, finishing well, and enjoying the journey.

Drs. Mark and Tom McCawley receiving the LANAP Protocol Gold Medal Award for their laser research from inventor Dr. Robert Gregg (left).

Bibliography

I've attempted to credit all the sources I could remember or recover. As I quoted Solomon, there are no new ideas. Some of these ideas I came up with on my own, and then discovered that others also had them. Many I borrowed from others. I've undoubtedly made a few *mess*takes. I apologize for any errors, or lack of reference to any person or thing, living or dead: it is purely unintentional. The following is a partial list of my chief resources. The ones marked with an asterisk are, in my opinion, the most valuable. The ones in bold type are the most recent.

Aesop's Fables. Barnes and Noble Classics. (500 BC) 2003.

Allen, James. As a Man Thinketh. (1903) Penguin. 2008.

*Bernstein, William J. If You Can: How Millennials Can Get Rich Slowly. Efficient Frontier Publications. 2014.

Bernstein, William J. The Investor's Manifesto: Preparing for Prosperity, Armageddon, and Everything in Between. Wiley. 2012.

Blue, Ron and Jeremy White. Surviving Financial Meltdown. Tyndale House Publishers. 2009.

Bogle, John C. Enough: True Measures of Money, Business, and Life. Wiley. 2008.

Bradberry, Travis and Jean Greaves. Emotional Intelligence 2.0. Talent Smart. 2009

Carlson, Richard. You Can be Happy No Matter What. New World Library. 1997.

*Carnegie, Dale. How to Stop Worrying and Start Living. Gallery Books. 2004.

Chaker, Anne Marie. The Strain the Covid Pandemic Is Putting on Marriages. The Wall Street Journal. August 4, 2020.

Chilton, David. The Wealthy Barber. Three Rivers Press. 1998

Cialdini, Robert. Pre-Suasion - A Revolutionary Way to Influence and Persuade. Simon and Schuster. 2016.

*Clason, George S. The Richest Man in Babylon. (1926) Best Success Books. 2008.

*Collier & Associates Doctors' Newsletter. collieradvisors. com. 2020.

*Coloroso, Barbara. Kids are Worth It! HarperCollins. 2002.

*Covey, Stephen R. The 7 Habits of Highly Effective People. Simon and Schuster. 1990.

Crowley, Chris and Henry Lodge. Younger Next Year: Live Strong, Fit, and Sexy-Until 80 and Beyond. Workman Publishing. 2007.

Dalai Lama. The Dalai Lama's Book of Wisdom. Thorsen's. 1999.

*Dawson, Peter and Gregg Lewis. A Better Way: The Surprising Path to a Complete Life. Widiom Publishing. 2018.

Dickens, Charles. A Christmas Carol. Ticknor and Fields.1843.

Dickens, Charles. David Copperfield. Tickner and Fields.1850.

Eker, Harv T. Secrets of a Millionaire Mind. HarperCollins. 2005.

Emmons, Robert A. Thanks! How the New Science of Gratitude Can Make You Happier. Houghton Mifflin. 2007.

Farran, Howard. Uncomplicate Business: All It Takes Is People, Time, and Money. Farran Enterprises. 2017.

Frankl, Viktor. Man's Search for Meaning: From Death-Camp to Existentialism, (1946). Beacon Press. 2006.

Galbreath, John Kenneth. A Short History of Financial Euphoria. Viking, Penguin. 1993.

*Gazelle, Gail. 7 Habits of Highly Resilient Physicians. August 6, 2020. KevinMD.com.

Gilbert, Daniel. Stumbling on Happiness. A. Knof. 2006.

Gladwell, Malcolm. Outliers. Little, Brown & Co. 2008.

*Goerig, Dr. Albert "Ace". Financial Freedom Blueprint. ACG Press. 2019.

*Gottman, John and Julie Schwartz Gottman. Eight Dates-Essential Conversations for a Lifetime of Love. Workman Publishing. 2018.

Gottman, John and Silver, Nan. The Seven Principles for Making Marriage Work. 1999. Used by permission of Crown Books, an imprint of Random House, a division of Penguin Random House
LLC. All rights reserved.

*Gottman, John and Julie Schwartz Gottman, Douglas Abrams, and Rachel Carlton Abrams. The Man's Guide to Women: Scientifically Proven Secrets from the Love Lab about What Women Really Want. 2016. Used by permission of Rodale Books, an imprint of Random House, a division of Penguin Random House LLC. All rights reserved.

Graham, Benjamin and Jason Zweig. The Intelligent Investor. Harper Collins. 2003.

Hsieh, Tony. Delivering Happiness. Grand Central Publishing. 2013.

Higgins, Tim. Pay for College Without Sacrificing Your Retirement. Bay Tree Publishing. 2008

Hill, Napoleon. Think and Grow Rich. Fawcett Crest Books. 1960.

*Housel, Morgan. The Psychology of Money: Timeless Lessons on Wealth, Greed, and Happiness. Harriman House. 2020.

Hurley, Joseph. Family Guide to College Savings. Bankrate, Inc. 2009. savingforcollege.com

*Jacobs, Gregg D., Ph.D. Say Good Night to Insomnia. Holt Paperbacks. 2009.

Kagan, Juli. Mind your Body - Pilates for the Seated Professional. Mind Body Publishing. 2008

Kellogg, Julie. Finish Strong. Simple Truths LLC. 2008.

Kiyosaki, Robert T. Rich Dad's Guide to Investing. Warner Business Books. 2000.

Kiyosaki, Robert T. Increasing your Financial IQ. Business Plus. 2008.

Kupperman, Joel. Six Myths About The Good Life-Thinking About What Has Value. Hackett Publishing, 2006.

Leiter, Michael and Christina Maslach. Banishing Burnout. Josey Bass. 2005.

Levitt, Stephen D. and Stephen J. Dubner. Super Freakonomics. HarperCollins. 2009.

Louvish, Simon. Coffee with Groucho. Duncan Baird. 2007.

*Lyubomirsky, Sonja. The Myths of Happiness: What Should Make You Happy, But Doesn't: What Shouldn't Make You Happy, But Does. Penguin Books. 2014.

MacKay, Charles. Extraordinary Popular Delusions and the Madness of Crowds. (1841) Wilder Publications. 2008.

Maslach, Christina. Burnout: The Cost of Caring. Malor. 2015.

Maslow, Abraham. Maslow on Management. John Wiley and Sons. 1998.

Matsen, Brad. Titanic's Last Secrets. Hachette Book Group. 2008.

McCawley,Thomas and Mark McCawley. A Clinician's Guide-Diagnosing and Treating Oral Diseases and Orofacial Pain. Bristlecone Publishing. 2017.

*McCawley, Tom and Mark McCawley. Saving Your Teeth, Implants and Your Health. Bristlecone Publishing. 2020.

*McCawley, Tom. The 4 Simple Secrets to Avoiding Life's BIG Financial *MESS*takes. Keynote, 2009.

McMahon, Susanna. The Portable Therapist. Dell Publishing. 1992.

*Mercer, Kendrick, and Albert Goering. Your Guide to Economic Freedom: Time and Money. ACGPress. 2004.

Nash, Laura and Howard Stevenson. Just Enough. John Wiley & Sons. 2004.

Opdyke, Jeff. Financially Ever After: The Couples Guide to Managing Money. HarperCollins. 2009.

Orman, Suze. The Ultimate Retirement Guide for 50+: Winning Strategies to Make Your Money Last a Lifetime. Hay House. 2020.

*Pankey, Lindsey D. and William J. Davis. A Philosophy of the Practice of Dentistry. Medical College Press. 1985.

*Peck, M. Scott. The Road Less Traveled. Simon & Schuster. 1978.

***Peterson, Jordan B. 12 Rules for Life: An Antidote to Chaos. Random House. 2018.**

Porras, Jerry, et al. Success Built to Last: Creating a Life That Matters. Wharton School Publishing. 2006.

*Ramsey, Dave. The Total Money Makeover. Thomas Nelson, Inc. 2013.

Rath,Tom. Are You Fully Charged? Silicon Guild. 2015.

Reeb, Lloyd. From Success to Significance: When the Pursuit of Success Isn't Enough. www.halftime.org.

***Robbins, Tony, and Peter Mallouk. Unshakeable: Your Financial Freedom Playbook. Simon and Schuster. 2017**

*Robin, Vicki, and Joe Dominguez. Your Money or Your Life. Penguin Press. 2008.

*Rogers, Jim. A Gift to My Children. Random House. 2009.
Roth, Benjamin. The Great Depression: A Diary. Perseus Books. 2010.

Rubin, Gretchen. The Happiness Project. HarperCollins. 2009.

Ruiz, Don Miguel. The Four Agreements. Amber-Allen. 1997.

Schuller, Robert H. Tough Times Never Last, But Tough People Do. Bantam Books, 1984.

Shiller, Robert. Irrational Exuberance. Random House. 2006.

Schuller, Robert H. Possibility Thinkers Bible: Proverbs (1000 BC). Nelson. 1982.

*Stanley, Thomas J. and William D. Danko. The Millionaire Next Door: The Surprising Secrets of America's Wealthy. Taylor Trade Publishing. 2010.

*Stein, Ben. The Capitalists Code: It Can Save Your Life and Make You Very Rich. Humanix Books. 2017.

Strain, Michael R. The American Dream is Not Dead. Templeton Press, 2020.

Swinney, Milton L. Stalag-IX-B: A Matter of Survival. Private Publication. 1999.

*The McGill Advisory Newsletter. www.BMHgroup.com. 2020.

*Tierney, John and Roy Baumeister. The Power of Bad. Penguin Press. 2019.

*Vaillant, George E. Triumphs of Experience. Harvard University Press. 2012.

Weintraub, Stanley. 11 Days in December-Christmas at the Bulge,1944. Free Press. 2006.

*Wilkinson, Bruce H. The Daily Walk Bible. Proverbs (1000 BC). New Living Translation, Tyndale House. 1997.

Zweig, Jason. Your Money and Your Brain. Simon & Schuster. 2007.

"But, my child, be warned:
There is no end of opinions ready to be expressed.
Studying them can go on forever,
and become very exhausting!"
Ecclesiastes 12:12

Tell me about it!

Image Credits

Blueprint Image. Cover, Title Page and Page xii. https://pixy.org/667/

A Christmas Carol. Page x. Wikipedia: https://en.wikipedia.org/wiki/File:A_Christmas_Carol_(1971_film).jpg

Marathon Finisher. Page xii. P2007 via iStock. https://www.istockphoto.com/vector/girl-crossing-the-finish-line-gm106576150-8606784

Man Reaching Summit. Pages 2 and 49. CoolClips.com

Mother Teresa, Calcutta, India. Page 7. Website: https://photoartinc.com/mother-teresa-calcutta-india

Morgue Resident Feet. Page 16. Theinkling via iStock. https://www.istockphoto.com/vector/morgue-resident-gm163818140-7292925

Coronavirus. Page 18. Lightspring via Shutterstock. https://www.shutterstock.com/image-illustration/coronavirus-outbreak-coronaviruses-influenza-background-dangerous-1621031059

Halfmoon Sleeping. Page 20. File:Sleep.svg. File svg wikimedia commons. https://webstockreview.net/images/clipart-moon-sleep.png

The Strain the COVID Pandemic is Putting on Marriages. Page 24. Wall Street Journal. August 5, 2020. ILLUSTRATION: JON KRAUSE. https://www.wsj.com/articles/the-strain-the-covid-pandemic-is-putting-on-marriages-11596551839

All My Eggs Were in One Basket. Page 33. CartoonStock.com

Fox and Chickens. Page 34. Unknown Author. CC BY-SA

Money Tree. Page 35. Alamy Stock Photo.

Rat Race. Page 36. CC BY-NC-ND.

The Ant and the Grasshopper. Page 38. http://kidsultimatezone.blogspot.com/2015/04/the-ant-and-grasshopper.html

Three Choices. Page 39. Created with images by Philippe Put - "sunish" - danielmoyle - "choices". https://spark.adobe.com/page/oWiS2royv3TSF/

Goose with a Golden Egg. Page 39. Alexum Photography via iStock.

Monarch butterfly on swamp milkweed in Michigan. Page 44. Photo by Jim Hudgins/USFWS.

Bedtime. Page 46. Annarki via iStock. https://www.istockphoto.com/vector/bedtime-gm122140521-9211513

Emoji. Page 61. https://picsart.com/i/sticker-hahas-285261536039211